The Alps

Books by W. A. Poucher
available from Constable

Scotland
Wales
The Lake District
The Highlands of Scotland
The magic of Skye
The Scottish Peaks
The Peak and Pennines
The Lakeland Peaks
The Welsh Peaks

Other books now out of print

The backbone of England
Climbing with a camera
Escape to the hills
A camera in the Cairngorms
Scotland through the lens
Highland holiday
The North Western Highlands
Lakeland scrapbook
Lakeland through the lens
Lakeland holiday
Lakeland journey
Over lakeland fells
Wanderings in Wales
Snowdonia through the lens
Snowdon holiday
Peak panorama
The Surrey hills
The magic of the Dolomites
West country journey
Journey into Ireland

The Weisshorn
from Blauherd

(frontispiece)

Blauherd is reached by the new tunnel to
Sunnegga and a small cablecar: in winter its ski-
slopes are the best in this area for teaching both
adults and children. The red-coated figures in
the foreground act as teachers in winter and as
mountain guides in summer. The picturesque
summit of the Weisshorn makes a perfect
background for this study.

THE ALPS

W. A. Poucher

Constable London

First published in Great Britain 1983
by Constable and Company Ltd
10 Orange Street London WC2H 7EG
Copyright © 1983 by W. A. Poucher
ISBN 0 09 465040 3
Reprinted 1987
Text filmset by Servis Filmsetting Ltd, Manchester
Printed and bound in Japan
by Dai Nippon Company, Tokyo

The photographs

4 The Weisshorn from Blauherd (frontispiece)
12/13 Mont Blanc from Megève
14/15 Chamonix
16 Le Brèvent
18/19 Mont Blanc from Le Brèvent
20/21 Plan Praz
22/23 The Aiguille du Midi
24/25 The Chamonix Aiguilles
26/27 The Aiguille Verte and Drus
28/29 The ridge of the Aiguilles Rouges
30 Climbing the Needle
32/33 Relaxing at La Flégère
34/35 The path to Lac Blanc
36/37 Lac Blanc
38/39 The Mer de Glace from Lac Blanc
40/41 Chardonnet from the Grands Montets
42/43 Aiguille d'Argentière
44/45 The Mer de Glace
46/47 The Plan de l'Aiguille
48 The Petit Dru
50/51 The Mer de Glace from the Signal
52/53 The Grands Charmoz
54/55 Walkers on the Mer de Glace
56 The Aiguille du Midi from the Mont Blanc tunnel
57 The Aiguille du Midi
58 The north peak
60/61 The Aiguilles du Plan and Verte
62/63 The finest subject from the platform
64/65 Looking south from the middle peak
66/67 Mont Blanc from the Midi-Geant cableway
68/69 The Peuterey ridge from Helbronner
70/71 Mont Blanc from the air
72/73 The Chamonix Aiguilles at sunset
74 The Wetterhorn from Grindelwald
75 First
76/77 Mannlichen
78 The Eiger
80/81 The train leaving Kleine Scheidegg for Jungfraujoch
82/83 Hard work
84/85 The Schilthorn
86/87 Piz Gloria
88/89 The Jungfrau group
90 The Gemmi from Leukerbad

91 Climbing the Wall
92/93 What are they looking at?
94/95 The Daubensee
96/97 The Balmhorn
98/99 Piz Bernina
100/101 The Cresta Run
102/103 The Bob Run
104/105 Zermatt
106 Flowers everywhere
108/109 The Square
110/111 The Matterhorn
112 The Gornergrat
114/115 Skiers at the Gornergrat
116/117 The Weisshorn
118 The ascent of the Mettelhorn
120/121 The Zinalrothorn
122/123 The Pulpit
124/125 The Obergabelhorn
126/127 A near view of the peaks
128/129 The three peaks from Zinal
130/131 The Dent Blanche
132/133 The Vier Eselsgrat
134/135 The Matterhorn from the summit of the Dent
        Blanche
136/137 The Dent d'Herens
138/139 The Matterhorn from Riffelalp
140/141 Schwarzsee
142 The Matterhorn from the air
144/145 Mountain transport of long ago
146/147 Looking east from the Belvedere Hotel
148/149 The Solvay Hut
150/151 The north face of the Roof
152/153 The summit cross
154/155 The Roof from the east
156/157 The Roof from the west
158/159 The summit ridge from the south
160/161 Monte Rosa from above the Matterhorn
162/163 The Gandegg Hut
164/165 Sunrise from Furgg
166/167 Kleine Matterhorn
168 Wind
170/171 The Breithorn
172/173 The Gornergrat from the Breithorn
174/175 Castor and Pollux
176/177 Lyskamm
178/179 The icy summit ridge of Lyskamm
180/181 Monte Rosa
182/183 Monte Rosa from Schwarzsee
184/185 The Margherita Hut
186/187 The Rimpfischhorn and Strahlhorn
188/189 The route of ascent
190/191 The Strahlhorn

192/193 The Mischabel chain from the south
194/195 The group from the west
196/197 The Taschhorn
198/199 Climbers on the Dom
    200 Zermatt from the air
202/203 The Matterhorn at sunset

Preface

During the last thirty years I have visited
Alpine resorts every year, and sometimes twice
a year – for climbing in the summer and ski-ing
in winter. I have always carried two Leicas (one
for Kodachrome and the other for
monochrome) and in recent years a Leicaflex,
together with a variety of lenses. In favourable
weather I took innumerable photographs, with
the result that my study now contains thousands
of subjects. From them I have chosen the
hundred pictures contained in this book.

In my early days it was only the mountaineer
who could enjoy the most magnificent of the
panoramas – the glittering vistas of snow and
ice opened up by the highest viewpoints.
Today, cablecars lift one easily to many of the
best vantage-points, so the visitor can share the
rewards of the climber without the effort – or
the risk!

It is a good thing for athletic youth to
measure its strength against these great
mountains, and for elderly climbers, mountain-
walkers and scramblers to know their
limitations. In making my selection for this
book, I have borne in mind the fact that many
readers may be walkers rather than climbers,
and have noted the best of the viewpoints
which can usually be reached by anyone who is
fit. The only exceptions are the close-ups of the
4000-metre summits which were taken during
several helicopter flights. To secure the unique
shot looking down on the Matterhorn, with
Monte Rosa in the background, the pilot had to
take the helicopter up to well over 5000 metres.
Mountaineers may argue with my choice of
viewpoints, in some cases, but they were always
arrived at with a view to absolute safety.

The Alps, ranks of jagged, snowy peaks
rising thousands of metres into the sky, are one
of the natural wonders of the world. They
induce a sense of wonder and of awe in
everyone who gazes on them, whether from an
alp, a cablecar, or the pages of a book.

W. A. Poucher
4 Heathfield
Reigate Heath
Surrey
1983

Mont Blanc from Megève

Travellers to Chamonix from Geneva get their first view of the Mont Blanc range on reaching Sallanches, but nowadays buildings spoil it. After exploring the neigbourhood, I decided that Megève was a better coign of vantage. In this photograph, the enormous bulk of Mont Blanc dwarfs the fine rock peaks extending to its left, beyond which lies the Col de Balme on the Swiss frontier. To the right (but out of this picture) the range continues to the Dome de Miage.

Chamonix

(overleaf)

I first came to Chamonix on a week's leave during World War I, and the town was then quiet and charming, with fields on each side of the road to the station. Today it is a bustling holiday resort, with parked cars and new buildings everywhere: the largest and most important mountaineering centre in Europe, with cablecars on either side of town which lift the visitor quickly to lofty viewpoints revealing the splendour of this gigantic ice-world. From the large telescope near the bridge over the River Arve, viewers hope to see climbers ascending the great white peak that dominates the town.

Le Brèvent *(2526m)*

This conspicuous rocky promontory, a viewpoint of undisputed excellence, rises to the north of Chamonix at the western end of the Aiguilles Rouges. It unveils a wonderful panorama of Mont Blanc, its satellites, and the Bossons and Teconnaz glaciers which fall almost to the road in the valley. While a few climbers attain the summit of Le Brèvent on foot by one of the two paths, it is usually reached by cablecar, with a change at Plan Praz.

Mont Blanc from Le Brèvent
(overleaf)

This is the world-famous view of Mont Blanc, taking in all its satellites. From left to right they are: Mt Blanc du Tacul, 4248m; Mt Maudit, 4465m; Mt Blanc, 4807m; Dome du Gouter, 4303m; Aiguille du Gouter, 3863m. The route of ascent from the Grands Mulets, 3051m, goes up to the left of the peak, and from St Gervais keeps to the skyline on the right.

Plan Praz *(2026m)*

In this photograph, the car is seen leaving Plan
Praz for Le Brèvent.

The Aiguille du Midi (3842m)

(overleaf)

This, the first peak to the east of the Mont Blanc group, is now reached by téléphérique, which, when it was built, was the highest in the world. Once, when I was descending to Plan Praz by way of the Col du Brèvent, the valley and main chain were curtained by cloud. Then, quite suddenly, it parted to unveil the Midi, a scene of great mountain beauty, as seen in this photograph.

The Chamonix Aiguilles

These splendid granite spires are the delight of
the rock-climber and are seen at their best from
Plan Praz. From left to right they are: Grepon,
3482m; Blaitière, 3522m; Plan, 3673m; with
Midi on the extreme right. They rise from the
Plan de l'Aiguille, which is reached by
téléphérique from Chamonix.

The Aiguille Verte (4122m) and Drus (3754m)

(overleaf)

These magnificent peaks rise to the east of the Mer de Glace and are seen at their finest from La Flégère, 1890m, which is easily reached from La Praz by cablecar. The ascent of these peaks is one of the most difficult in the whole range.

The ridge of the Aiguilles Rouges

This broken ridge extends eastwards from Le Brèvent, and its traverse should only be made by experienced mountain-walkers. A sketchy track winds in and out along its crest, where every care is necessary.

Climbing
the Needle

This vertical rock is a conspicuous feature of
the Aiguilles Rouges, and is not unlike Britain's
Napes Needle, save that it is much larger. It is a
tricky scramble to reach a good viewpoint, and
by the time I had found one, the other climbers
had reached the top.

Relaxing at La Flégère (1890m)

Below the ridge track there is a splendid path
running along a wooded shelf from Plan Praz
to La Flégère, where rest and good food may
be enjoyed. Sunning myself on the terrace one
afternoon, I took this picture as a change from
the scenic beauty of its surroundings.

The path to Lac Blanc

Small cablecars rise from La Flégère to Index at
2385m, from which one of the finest walks in
this area may be taken along a stony track that
reveals many beautiful scenes – including the
first view of Chardonnet, 3824m, and
Argentière, 3900m, the last two important peaks
in the Mont Blanc range.

Lac Blanc

(overleaf)

This attractive little lake is the usual terminus of the walk from Index, and lies below the highest summit of the Aiguilles Rouges. Enclosed on three sides by steep crags, it is open to the south, where a chalet-hotel stands on the edge of the water; and it opens up extensive views of the main chain. A mule-track, descending at an easy gradient to La Flégère, is the best way back to the cablecar.

The Mer de Glace from Lac Blanc

(overleaf pp 38/39)

Just below the lake is a well-cairned platform – the ideal viewpoint hereabouts. Amongst the vast array of peaks of the main chain opposite lies the Mer de Glace; the platform gives a bird's-eye-view of its twisting course.

Chardonnet from the Grands Montets (3297m)

This magnificent viewpoint is reached from Croix de Lognan (about 1 km below Argentière on the Chamonix side) by téléphérique, which rises 2030m in 15 minutes, with a change at the half-way station, 1972m. On reaching the summit, there is a striking view to the east of Aig. Chardonnet, as seen in this picture: and also wonderful vistas of Mont Blanc, the Chamonix Aiguilles, the double summit of the Drus, and the tremendous ice wall of the Aiguille Verte.

Aiguille d' Argentière *(3900m)*

Adjoining Chardonnet, this peak offers some of
the best snow-climbing in the region.

The Mer de Glace
(1913m)

(overleaf)

Like the Matterhorn, this glacier must be well known to millions of people. Brought by the rack-railway to Montenvers, crowds gather round the hotel, shops, and elevated restaurant to gaze in wonder at the long river of ice below.

The Plan de l' Aiguille

There is more to be seen by walking to
Montenvers from the Plan station on the Midi
téléphérique. Below the towers and spires of the
Chamonix Aiguilles there is a broad shelf, along
which run two paths. The mountain-walker
should keep to the lower one, as the other runs
at the base of the peaks and involves crossing
two glaciers.

The Petit Dru (3754m)

The path eventually rises up the hillside, and at the top discloses a marvellous view of this granite obelisk, whose ascent is one of the many difficult climbs on the main chain.

The Mer de Glace from the Signal

(overleaf)

A rough ridge known as the Crete des Charmoz extends to the right of this belvedere, and just below it lies the ideal viewpoint for the Mer de Glace, as seen in this picture. It is known locally as the Signal, and the view not only pleases the eye by the absence of buildings, but also reveals the encircling peaks to perfection.

The Grands Charmoz *(3444m)*

From the Signal, there is also a splendid view
of this famous peak, with the sunlight catching
the detached summit of the République, 3305m.

Walkers on the Mer de Glace

(overleaf)

There is easy access to the glacier from Montenvers, and those who walk along it will perhaps be surprised at its roughness. They should keep well away from the crevasses. If bound for the Couvercle Hut, experienced mountain-walkers will not be deterred by the ladders and rails on the steep rock-face of Les Egralets.

The Aiguille du Midi from the Mont Blanc tunnel

(overleaf p56)

This photograph shows the entrance to the tunnel, together with the very top of the Aiguille du Midi. The tunnel is 11.6 km long – the longest in the world – and connects Chamonix with Courmayeur, passing 2480m under the Midi. It takes about 20 minutes to drive through it.

The Aiguille du Midi *(3842m)*

(overleaf p 57)

Before 1955, no one but an experienced mountaineer could reach this lofty summit and revel in the superb panorama that is unfolded on a clear day. But in that year the téléphérique to its north peak was opened, followed in 1958 by an extension to Pointe Helbronner on the Italian frontier. This made it possible for any tourist to enjoy the splendours of the mountain world – without exerting himself! This picture, showing the cablecar approaching the north summit, was taken from a stance on the very edge of the snow, where the drop was around 600m.

The north peak

Visitors taking the cablecar to its terminus
(shown in this picture) should beware of the
sudden change in atmospheric pressure. The car
rises 1278m in 8 minutes to the first station on
the Plan de l'Aiguille; and on the second
section, which is very steep near the top (see
previous picture) rises 1472m in 6 minutes,
making a total rise of 2750m in about 20
minutes. While experienced climbers are not
unduly affected by this quick rise in altitude, I
have twice helped carry out passengers who had
collapsed before reaching the top.

The Aiguilles du Plan and Verte

When the visitor has become accustomed to the change in atmospheric pressure, he should walk up to the platform above the station, which discloses a magnificent panorama. The eye is drawn immediately to the Chamonix Aiguilles, of which Plan seems so near at hand; and to the many receding clouded pinnacles which terminate with the more lofty Verte, as seen in this picture.

The finest subject from the platform

(overleaf)

The marvelling visitor to the north peak platform finally focuses on the group of peaks beyond the Vallée Blanche, with the Grands Jorasses, 4208m, on the left and the Aiguille du Geant, 4013m, on the right. It is only in this direction that a good photographic foreground can be discovered – the snowy ridge on the right corner leading down to the Vallée, which would be improved by figures with skis.

Looking south from the middle peak

The middle peak is the highest of the Midi peaks, opening up an unrestricted view in all directions: this view to the south, above the lower south peak, reveals a splendid prospect of the Gran Paradiso National Park in Italy. (Being more than 30m higher than its northern neighbour, it gives a view towards Mont Blanc that is even finer.) But the summit platform of the middle peak itself is marred by a television transmission aerial in the centre.

Mont Blanc from the Midi-Geant cableway

(overleaf)

The cableway that crosses the Mont Blanc range from the Aiguille du Midi is more than 5 km long, and the half-hour journey to Pointe Helbronner offers one of the most exciting experiences that the mountain-lover can enjoy. The cabins usually move in threes; each one holds four people and has a half-open window on the Mont Blanc side which will accept a miniature camera and lens. The first span crosses the Vallée Blanche to Gros Rognon, a small peak projecting from the glacier, which is an invaluable support for the long cable. The next span crosses the Geant Glacier to Pointe Helbronner. As the car moves along slowly, the scene changes dramatically, and in this photograph it reveals the Grand Capucin and Mont Blanc. The Tour Ronde is just out of the picture to the left.

The Peuterey ridge from Helbronner

The finest scene disclosed at the end of the
cableway is the Peuterey ridge rising to the
dominating peak beyond the Brenva face of the
mountain. Aiguille Noire is the sharp peak on
the left, and the notoriously difficult Dames
Anglaises in the gap on its right.

Mont Blanc from the air

This shot was taken on a commercial flight
from Geneva to Nice.

The Chamonix Aiguilles at sunset

(overleaf)

On a clear winter evening these peaks blaze like red beacons in the sky; this photograph of them makes a fitting close to the series of the magnificent Mont Blanc range.

The Wetterhorn (*3701m*) from Grindelwald (*1034m*)

(overleaf p 74)

This beautiful village is easily reached by train from Interlaken or by road from Berne, and is a splendid centre for the exploration of the Bernese Oberland. The Wetterhorn dominates the village, as shown here, but is seen to greater advantage from the lofty viewpoint of First, which can be reached from Grindelwald by chairlift.

First (*2168m*)

(overleaf p 75)

This excellent viewpoint, reached in 30 minutes by chairlift from Grindelwald, opens up a magnificent panorama of the main chain from the Wetterhorn to the Eiger. In winter it is a first-class ski-ing centre; in summer it offers many beautiful walks, in particular the one from Schynige Platte by way of the Foulhorn, 2684m. This picture of the distant Foulhorn was taken from a point above the terminus of the chairlift.

Mannlichen (*2343m*)

(overleaf pp 76/77)

In my early days the only way to reach this peak was on ski from Kleine Scheidegg, but some years ago a cableway was opened from Wengen, and more recently a 9-km cableway was built from Grindelwald. Mannlichen yields the finest panorama of the Eiger, Monch, and the Jungfrau, and the plateau below it permits the landing of small aircraft – as seen in this picture.

71

The Eiger (3970m)

The precipitous 1524-m limestone wall of this peak is world-famous for the many attempts to climb it, and for the many accidents and rescues that have taken place there. An Austro-German party was the first to reach the top, in 1938. Visitors can examine the face in detail by using the powerful telescope at the hotel on Kleine Scheidegg, or may prefer to leave the train at Alpiglen for a closer view.

The train leaving Kleine Scheidegg for Jungfraujoch (3454m)

(overleaf)

The scene in this photograph is dominated by the Eiger and Monch, and the train passes through both of them in an 8-km tunnel on its way to Jungfraujoch, the highest station in Europe. Jungfraujoch is the lofty col lying between the Jungfrau and the Monch at the head of the Aletsch Glacier, the longest in the Alps.

Hard work

I was returning from the SAC Scharoarzegg
Hut, 2485m, in the summer of 1963, when I
met this man near Stieregg on his way to make
some repairs. Nowadays his load would
probably be taken by helicopter.

The Schilthorn
(2971m)

(overleaf)

This peak rises above Murren and is attained by the longest cableway (6870m) in the Alps. It starts at Stechelberg in the Lauterbrunnen valley, and is easily reached by bus and car throughout the year. Berg at 2677m, where visitors change cablecars, has a large sun-terrace which gives the first good view of the Jungfrau group. This shot was taken at Berg, and shows the cable rising to the summit of the Schilthorn.

Piz Gloria

Standing on the summit of the Schilthorn, this restaurant revolves on its own axis to reveal a beautiful prospect of the surrounding Alps. In summer it is the starting point of many walks, and in winter of a long ski-run.

The Jungfrau group
(overleaf)

Taken from the Piz Gloria, this photograph reveals the famous group of peaks. From left to right they are: Eiger, 3970m; Monch, 4099m; and Jungfrau, 4158m.

The Gemmi from Leukerbad
(overleaf p 90)

The Gemmi is a mountain pass of great beauty, connecting the Valais with the Bernese Oberland. Walkers who decide to make this expedition should start from Leukerbad, taking a cablecar to the beginning of the high pass at 2350m – thus avoiding the ascent of the Wall (seen in this picture) which, however, is threaded by a sensational path. The pass ends at Stock, where another cablecar gives easy access to Kandersteg. If this transport is used at both ends, the walk can be completed in a leisurely 5 hours.

Climbing the Wall
(overleaf p 91)

I made this ascent on only one occasion; it took about an hour to reach the top, where it revealed some sensational views.

What are they looking at?
(overleaf pp 92/93)

This shot was taken from the top of the Wall where, on a clear day, there is marvellous panorama of the Alps extending from the Dom to Mont Blanc. However, although I waited there on several occasions, the atmosphere was never clear enough to do justice to the scene.

The Daubensee

This beautiful lake comes into view soon after
starting the Gemmi walk, with glimpses of the
surrounding peaks on either hand.

The Balmhorn
(3700m)
(overleaf)

On approaching the Berghotel Schwarenbach at 2061m, this elegant peak comes into view. It is easily climbed in summer from the hotel, (seen in the picture), and other interesting excursions can safely be made from here as well.

Piz Bernina (4049m)
(overleaf pp 98/99)

The highest peak in the Engadine, Piz Bernina is flanked by Piz Palu, 3905m, and Piz Roseg, 3937m. The finest viewpoint for them all is Diavolezza, 2978m, which may be reached all year round by a cablecar whose valley station is on the Bernina Pass into Italy. During the summer it is the starting point for many spectacular walks and climbs, and in winter for long ski-runs.

The Cresta Run

The first Cresta Run was built in 1884 by a
small party of Englishmen who were being
treated in St Moritz for asthma and
tuberculosis. At that time the Cresta riders were
the fastest in the world, but nowadays the
1200m ice gully which ends at Celerina is
usually done faster, at more than 80 kph (the
record is 145 kph). In this picture, the Cresta
rider is taking the notorious bends of the
Shuttlecock, the greatest test of his skill.

The Bob Run

This famous run is near the Cresta and passes
through a heavily wooded area. Here the
bobsleigh is seen at the difficult bend above the
road, thundering along the vertical ice wall
before taking a steep left-hand bend below the
road.

Zermatt

(overleaf)

During the last thirty years I have returned
again and again to Zermatt, and the reason for
my preference is its retention of much of its
original character. The complete absence of
motor cars, its church, climbers' graveyard,
shops, and hotels, endow the village with a very
special charm. But do the thousands of tourists
come for the village or the Matterhorn? With
the rapid development of mountaineering
started here by the English, the answer is surely
that Zermatt was bound to become an
important resort, since it is surrounded by more
4000-m peaks than any other village in the
Alps.

Flowers everywhere

Among the attractions of Zermatt is the
wonderful profusion of flowers decorating its
chalets and hotels, which delights the visitor.

The Square

The comings and goings of both natives and
visitors centre on the great open space in front
of the Catholic church, with many little shops
and bars opposite.

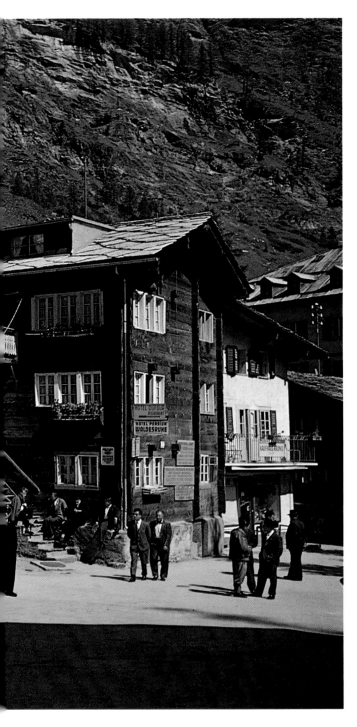

The Matterhorn
(4478m)

(overleaf)

Where should the new visitor go who is anxious to see this famous mountain and not merely glimpse its summit above the Zermatt houses? The nearest point that discloses the whole peak to perfection is Winkelmatten, as seen in this photograph. It can be reached in half an hour by first crossing the bridge below the church and then taking the second turn to the right. The walk begins steeply but soon becomes an easy gradient. On arrival at the hamlet, coffee may be taken at one of two restaurants while gazing on this magnificent peak.

The Gornergrat
(3130m)

The cog railway to this famous belvedere was
opened in 1898 and carries the passenger to one
of the most spectacular viewpoints in the Alps.
Visitors who stay in Zermatt for only a few
days should make this their first excursion, for
from the Kulm Hotel terrace they will see
several of the highest mountains in the region
(including the Matterhorn, as seen here), the
whole scene a glittering world of ice and snow.

Skiers at the Gornergrat

This shot shows the starting point of a famous
ski-run near the station. The mountains in the
background are the Dent Blanche on the left
and the Obergabelhorn on the right.

The Weisshorn
(4505m)
(overleaf)

This dramatically beautiful peak stands at the north-western end of the mountain chain encircling Zermatt, and looks its best from the Unterrothorn on the other side of the valley. It is flanked on the left by the Schalihorn, 3974m, as shown in this photograph. The Weisshorn is ascended from Randa and it takes from 4 to 5 hours to reach the hut, whence the peak is climbed by its eastern ridge, on the right. It is usually descended by the same ridge.

The ascent of the Mettelhorn
(3406m)

This photograph was taken about half-way up
the climb from Zermatt to the Mettelhorn, from
a point where the track leaves the path to the
Rothorn Hut. The mule-path threads a steep
gorge from Zermatt and passes the Trift Hotel,
which is seen near the base of this picture with
Monte Rosa and Lyskamm on the distant
skyline. The Mettelhorn, which yields a
spectacular view of the Weisshorn, should only
be climbed by those who are very fit, as it takes
at least 12 hours there and back.

The Zinalrothorn
(4221m)

(overleaf)

The long twisting ridge of this mountain is
disclosed against its shadowed summit, as seen
in this view from the Unterrothorn. The peak is
usually climbed from the Rothorn Hut, which
lies below the ridge and is reached from
Zermatt in about 5 hours.

The Pulpit

It is difficult even to reach the spectacular
narrow ridge, known as the Pulpit, that rises
steeply to the true summit of the Zinalrothorn;
and its ascent, with terrific drops on either side,
is the final thrill of the long climb from the hut.
There is a glimpse of the Weisshorn on the
right of this picture.

The Obergabelhorn
(4063m)

(overleaf)

From any point on the eastern side of the
Zermatt valley this graceful peak commands
attention, but it looks its finest from Sunnegga,
directly opposite. In winter it makes a better
picture than in summer, when the greens and
browns below the snowline detract from its
beauty. On its right stands the Wellenkuppe,
3903m, and on its left the rock ridge of the
Untergabelhorn, 3892m.

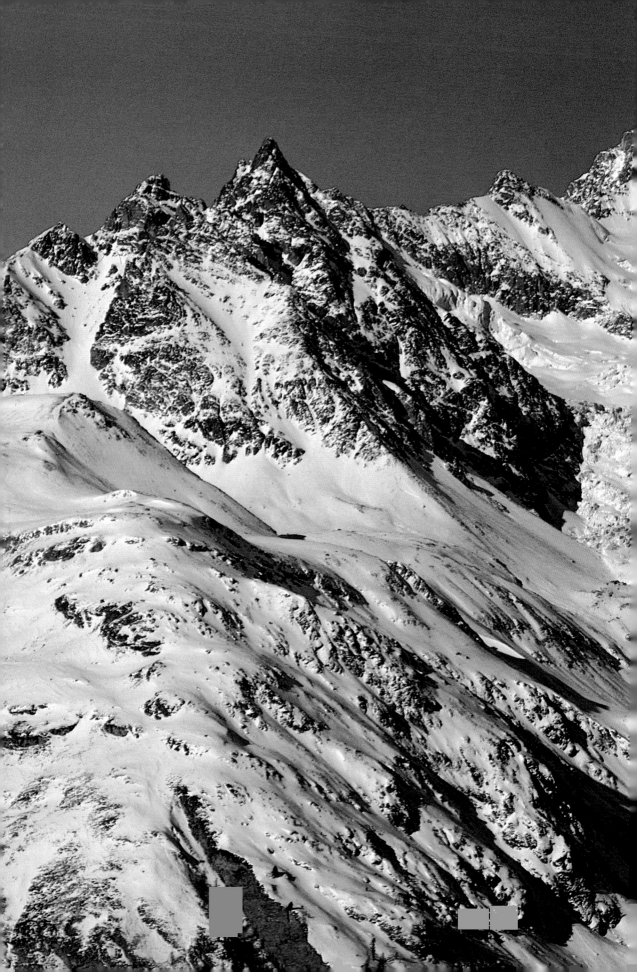

A near view of the peaks

The ascent of the Obergabelhorn can be made most easily by the traverse of the Untergabelhorn, but the usual route starts from the Rothorn Hut. The Wellenkuppe is first climbed by its east ridge, mainly over snow, followed by the narrow snow ridge seen in this photograph, where the upper section is extremely steep and is the most difficult and sensational part of the ascent.

The three peaks from Zinal

(overleaf)

I wanted to see the western aspect of the three previous peaks, and so took this shot of them from an unnamed mountain in the Val d'Anniviers. But neither the Weisshorn on the left, the Zinalrothorn in the centre, nor the Obergabelhorn on the right display such a splendid elevation as we have seen in the previous pages.

The Dent Blanche (4357m)

(overleaf pp 130/131)

This mountain is clearly seen from any point between Trockener Steg and Schwarzsee, and looks its best when its riven southern front is snowbound. This study of it was taken from the old cableway station.

The Vier Eselsgrat

This ridge is the most popular route for
ascending the Dent Blanche and it starts from
the Schonbiel Hut, 2694m, which is reached by
a 4-hour walk from Zermatt. It is famous for
the striking, foreshortened view of the
Matterhorn on the other side of the Zmutt
Glacier; and from it the sketchy moraine track
rises to the Dent Blanche.

The cairn on this peak is almost directly above the Schonbiel Hut, so the view of the Matterhorn from both places is similar, except that the lower view is foreshortened. In the photograph, the snowy Zmutt Ridge can be seen below the centre of the vast, shadowed rock triangle.

The Dent d'Herens (4171m)

This peak is seldom seen by the mountain-walker, because it is hidden behind the Matterhorn: the finest view of it is from the summit of the Dent Blanche, as seen in this photograph. On its right lies the Col d'Herens, a famous glacier route to Arolla on the high-level ski-run from Chamonix to Zermatt and Saas Fee.

The Matterhorn from Riffelalp

(overleaf)

This peak is so dominant when seen from most places that it is not easy to pick the finest viewpoint. Many mountain-walkers would choose the Riffelsee, provided that the mountain's reflection in the lake was unruffled; but my preference is for this shot from Riffelalp. It was taken from the lofty path which ultimately joins the main route to Grunsee beyond the railway, and photographers should note that they have to step down from it to ensure the inclusion of the whole mountain.

Schwarzsee

The tiny lake seen in this photograph lies immediately below the prominent Hornli ridge of the Matterhorn. It has probably been admired by more people than any lake in the Alps, and on a sunny day many of them walk down from the nearby cablecar station to see the little Chapel of Maria zum Schnee, built on its northern shore in 1780. There are marvellous views of the surrounding peaks – in this picture, the Obergabelhorn is dominant. Most visitors return to Zermatt by cablecar, but strong walkers return by way of Staffelalp, using a good path which yields a remarkable retrospect of the Matterhorn.

The Matterhorn from the air

This photograph was taken from a helicopter flying above Schwarzsee and clearly shows the Zermatt route of ascent, from start to finish. In good weather the climb takes about 5 hours.

Mountain transport of long ago

Taken in my early days, this shot has been
included because mule-transport has now largely
been replaced by helicopter. In those days it
took about 5 hours to walk from Zermatt to
the old hut at the foot of the climb, whereas
today it takes only about 2 hours from the
Schwarzsee cablecar station.

Looking east from the Belvedere Hotel

(overleaf)

This photograph, opening up a wide panorama from the Gornergrat to the Breithorn, always reminds me of the steep, zigzagging path, with its seemingly endless 42 bends, that finishes at the door of this hotel. The walk to this point from Schwarzsee may be undertaken by anyone who is fit, and, eating lunch on the hotel terrace on a clear day, the walker can revel in this stupendous view.

The Solvay Hut

(4003m)
(overleaf pp 148/149)

This remarkable hut is situated below the Shoulder of the Matterhorn, and occupies one of the few flat breaks in the narrow ridge. In the event of an accident on, or near, the Roof, the climber can receive attention here until he is transferred to a helicopter for rapid transport to hospital.

The north face of the Roof

On reaching the Shoulder, the climber is faced
with the ascent of this formidable rock wall,
where fixed ropes help him attain the
Matterhorn's summit ridge. It was during the
descent of the Roof that the notorious accident
happened to Whymper's party in 1865: he and
his two guides, Taugwalder and son, survived,
while four others lost their lives.

The summit cross

(overleaf)

A closer view of the ridge pictured on the previous page shows the summit cross more clearly.

The Roof from the east

The steepness of this enormous rock wedge will
be appreciated after seeing this photograph.

The Roof from the west

This shot shows the end point of the climb
from Italy

The summit ridge from the south

In this shot, climbers can be seen walking along the ridge towards the cross. It should be noted that while the Zermatt ridge gives the most popular ascent of the Matterhorn, there are three others which are more difficult: Furgg-grat on the left edge of the east face; Nordwand on the north face; and Zmuttgrat, the snow ridge on the extreme right. (There are still other routes on the Italian side.) Nordwand, first climbed in 1931, is considered the most difficult and dangerous because of its verticality, the instability of rock and snow, and falling stones.

Monte Rosa
from above
the Matterhorn

(overleaf)

Our helicopter had to be taken to well over 5000m to secure this unique photograph, with the Zermatt ridge in shadowed profile and Monte Rosa in the far distance.

The Gandegg Hut *(3029m)*

This well-known inn, patronized alike by climbers and mountain-walkers, was reached on foot in my early days, and was about 5 hours from Zermatt. Today it takes only about half an hour to reach it Trockener Steg. In those days it was the base for the ascent of the Breithorn but since the opening of the cablecar to Kleine Matterhorn, it is easier and quicker to make the ascent of the Breithorn from there.

Sunrise from Furgg *(2431m)*

The cablecar from Trockener Steg is just
arriving at Furgg station, and the rays of the
rising sun impart a strange brilliance to the
overhead cables.

Kleine Matterhorn
(3883m)

(overleaf)

Work on the cableway to this little peak began
in 1976 and was completed in 1979; it is the
highest cableway in the world, exceeding that of
the Aiguille du Midi by some 20m. The
problems involved in its construction were
immense, and included a cable-span of 2885m
from the pylon above the Gandegg Hut to its
station on the precipitous face of the mountain.
The main object was to develop summer skiing,
and this has already proved a great success. But
until the panoramic platform is open to the
public, it will not be possible to see the
stupendous view of all the 4000m peaks above
Zermatt.

Wind

Neither climber nor skier would wish to be anywhere near Kleine Matterhorn in the windy conditions seen in this photograph. When it was taken, the line was closed because of the risk of an accident to any car crossing the swaying cable below the top station.

The Breithorn (4160m)

(overleaf)

This great mountain rises from the glacier directly opposite the Gornergrat, and is seen at its best in either early morning or late evening.

The Gornergrat from the Breithorn

Taken from the Breithorn summit, this picture
shows the Gornergrat beyond the glacier with
the Mischabel chain on the skyline. In good
weather a guide supervises an easy climb to the
summit of the Breithorn daily, starting from the
Kleine Matterhorn.

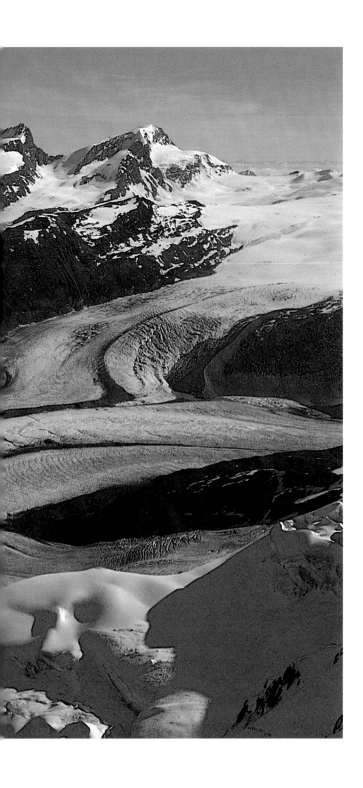

Castor and Pollux *(4226m and 4091m)*

Taken from the Gornergrat, this photograph
shows the two minor peaks that rise between
the Breithorn and Lyskamm.

Lyskamm (4527m)

(overleaf)

This mountain is also well seen from the Gornergrat terrace, rising on the right of Monte Rosa.

The icy summit ridge of Lyskamm

(overleaf pp 178/179)

The traverse of this ridge is usually made from the Monte Rosa Hut, and this remarkable photograph, taken from Monte Rosa, reveals its great difficulties.

Monte Rosa (4634m)

The classic view of the great snow mountain, this picture was taken from the Gornergrat. Dufourspitze is the higher of the two summits, Nordend being 4609m. The ascent is always made from the Monte Rosa Hut, 2795m, which is sited above the spectacular junction of two glaciers. The hut can be reached from Rotenboden station on the Gornergrat railway, and the walk, a relatively easy one for the ordinary pedestrian, crosses the Gornerglacier by a marked route.

Monte Rosa from Schwarzsee

(overleaf)

This is my favourite view of the mountain, because it includes a glimpse of the glacier with the Riffelhorn, 2927m, frowning upon it on the left. This small peak is only a few steps from Rotenboden Station, and its cliffs, facing the glacier, are a training ground for anyone who aspires to scale the Matterhorn.

The Margherita Hut (4556m)

The highest and most remote in the district,
this hut is on the Italian frontier to the east of
Monte Rosa. It was rebuilt in 1980 and stands
on the edge of a cliff amid a sea of blinding
snow. In any emergency on the summits nearby,
this is the only hut within reach.

The Rimpfischhorn and Strahlhorn

(overleaf)

Coming now to the Mischabel chain, we see
these two peaks at their best in winter from the
Unterrothorn, as shown in this picture.

The route of ascent

The Rimpfischhorn, 4199m, is usually climbed from Flualp, 2610m, seen in this picture: it involves a long walk over snow, followed by an easy rock ridge of about 300m.

The Strahlhorn *(4190m)*

The guide and his client are here seen on the
summit of the peak, which is sometimes
climbed from the Britannia Hut above Saas Fee.

The Mischabel chain from the south

(overleaf)

It is not easy for mountain-walkers to find a perfect viewpoint for this group, and in these circumstances I suggest the Unterrothorn, from where the great triangular Taschhorn rises on the right of the chain, as seen here. In winter the snow adds to the beauty of the scene.

The group from the west

This shot was taken from near the Mettelhorn,
and includes the flat-topped summit of Alphubel
on the right.

The Taschhorn (4490m)

Seen from near Alphubel, the dynamic southern façade of this mountain is in the foreground, with the Dom, 4545m, rising behind it and dominating the whole chain. The ascent of this face of the Taschhorn is one of the hardest in the group.

Climbers on
the Dom
(overleaf)

Many ascents in the Mischabel chain are made from the Dom Hut, 2928m, which lies some 5 hours above Randa. The path is very steep all the way, and includes the ascent of an easy rock-face. The climbers in this photograph are nearing the summit of the Dom.

Zermatt from the air

The picture shows the enclosed situation of this enchanting village.

The Matterhorn at sunset

(overleaf)

On a sunny summer evening a friend and I were sitting in the beautiful garden of the Zermatterhof Hotel when, glancing above the trees, we saw the rays of the setting sun reflected by the clouds forming on the Matterhorn. Said my friend, 'Let's go up to the Hornli Hut tomorrow, and climb the peak next day!' But the morrow brought bad weather and we never went. In a way I was glad – for in my 90th year I might not have been able even to reach the lofty Belvedere Hotel!